Saquon Barkley

From Penn State to NFL Glory for Kids

Kenton Powell

Copyright

All rights reserved. No part of this publication may be reproduced, distributed, or transmitted in any form or by any means, including photocopying, recording, and other electronic or mechanical methods, without prior written permission of the publisher, except in case of briefs quotation embodied in critical reviews and certain other noncommercial uses permitted by copyright law.

Copyright © Kenton Powell, 2025

Table of Contents

Introduction   4

Chapter 1: Growing Up in Pennsylvania   9

Chapter 2: High School Hero: Breaking Records and Winning Hearts   15

   College Stardom: Lighting Up the Big Ten   20

Chapter 3: Rookie of the Year: Taking the NFL by Storm   27

   Life Off the Field: Family, Fitness, and Fun   32

Fun Facts About Saquon Barkley   **38**

Football Drills Inspired by Saquon   44

Conclusion: Run Hard, Dream Big Like Saquon Barkley!   **55**

Introduction

Saquon Barkley is the kind of athlete who makes you stop and stare, wondering, "How does he *do* that?" Whether he's leaping over defenders, spinning out of tackles, or speeding down the field so fast it looks like everyone else is moving in slow motion, Saquon plays football like he was born for it. But his story didn't start on a fancy football field with thousands of cheering fans. It began in the bustling streets of

The Bronx, New York, where little Saquon dreamed big.

As a kid, Saquon's family meant everything to him. He looked up to his dad, Alibay, a former boxer, and his mom, Tonya, who worked hard to keep the family going. Saquon wasn't just surrounded by love—he was surrounded by inspiration. His uncles and brother played sports, and he wanted to be just like them. When his family moved to Pennsylvania, Saquon got his chance to shine. But it wasn't all smooth sailing. At first, he wasn't the team's biggest or fastest kid. He had to work for it. And that's where

Saquon's magic began—not in the touchdowns or trophies, but in how he kept pushing himself to improve daily.

By high school, Saquon was a force to be reckoned with. He wasn't just good—he was *unstoppable*. Colleges lined up to recruit him, but he chose Penn State University, a decision that would change his life forever. At Penn State, Saquon didn't just play football; he lit up the field. He broke records, wowed fans, and earned a reputation as one of the best college players in the country. NFL teams couldn't wait to get him, and in 2018, the New York Giants selected him as the second overall pick in the draft.

From that moment on, Saquon became a household name. He was named Rookie of the Year in his first season, dazzling fans with his powerful runs and fearless attitude. But Saquon isn't just about the highlights—he's about heart. He's faced challenges, including serious injuries, but he's always returned stronger. For Saquon, football is about more than just winning games. It's about inspiring others, proving that hard work pays off, and showing the world that no dream is too big.

Saquon Barkley's journey reminds us that greatness doesn't happen overnight. It takes grit, passion, and a belief in yourself—even when the odds are against you. Whether making history on the football field or giving back to his community, Saquon is a hero for kids everywhere who dare to dream big.

Chapter 1: Growing Up in Pennsylvania

When Saquon Barkley was a little kid, his family decided to leave The Bronx, New York's busy streets, and move to Bethlehem, Pennsylvania. It was a significant change—goodbye to the towering buildings and hello to quieter neighbourhoods and open fields. But for Saquon, it was also the start of something extraordinary.

In Pennsylvania, Saquon found himself surrounded by sports. His dad, Alibay, had been a boxer, and his family loved competition. But Saquon wasn't always the strongest or the fastest kid. When he first started playing sports, he wasn't exactly a superstar. He wasn't the kid everyone pointed to and said, "That one's going pro!" Instead, Saquon was just a kid who loved playing, even when things didn't come easy.

At first, Saquon spent more time watching his older brother, Ali, than playing. Ali was a star athlete in his own right, and Saquon admired him. He wanted to be just like him. But instead of just dreaming about it, Saquon decided to do something about it. He trained. He practised. He pushed himself harder and harder. And slowly but surely, something incredible started to happen.

By the time Saquon reached Whitehall High School, he had become a powerhouse athlete. He wasn't just playing football anymore—he was dominating. He could sprint like a cheetah and dodge defenders like invisible wings. He became the school's football team star, and people started to notice. College scouts came to his games, jaws dropping as Saquon weaved through defences like it was the easiest thing in the world. But Saquon wasn't just focused on football. He also ran track and played basketball, always working to become stronger, faster, and better.

Saquon's success didn't come without challenges. He didn't grow up with fancy training programs or endless resources. He had a family that believed in him and a determination that wouldn't quit. His dad was his biggest supporter, constantly reminding him that he could achieve anything if he worked. And Saquon took that advice to heart, working tirelessly to become the athlete he knew he could be.

By the end of high school, Saquon was a sensation. He ran for over 3,600 yards and scored 63 touchdowns in just two seasons. That's the kind of performance that makes college recruiters drool. But Saquon didn't let the attention go to his head. He stayed humble, focused, and determined to keep getting better.

Growing up in Pennsylvania wasn't just a chapter in Saquon Barkley's story—it was the foundation. It was where he learned that hard work beats talent when talent doesn't work hard. It's where he grew from a quiet kid with big dreams into a football phenom ready to take on the world. And as it turned out, the world wasn't prepared for the unstoppable force that was Saquon Barkley.

Chapter 2: High School Hero: Breaking Records and Winning Hearts

When Saquon Barkley arrived at Whitehall High School in Pennsylvania, he wasn't just another kid trying out for the football team. He was a kid with a dream—and the determination to make it come true. But even Saquon couldn't have predicted how much his hard work would pay off. By the time he left high school, he wasn't just the star of his team; he was a local legend, breaking records and capturing the hearts of everyone who watched him play.

At first, Saquon wasn't a superstar overnight. He had to prove himself. Early on, he worked relentlessly to get faster, stronger, and more brilliant on the field. He would spend hours training, running drills, and studying the game. It wasn't long before all that effort began to show. Suddenly, Saquon wasn't just good—he was terrific.

As a running back, Saquon seemed almost impossible to stop. Imagine trying to catch a lightning bolt or tackle a speeding train. That's what it was like for defenders when Saquon had the ball. He could burst through tiny gaps in the defence, spin past tacklers like a top, or flat-out outrun everyone on the field. And if that wasn't enough, he could leap over defenders like they were hurdles.

In his junior and senior years, Saquon's stats were mind-blowing. He rushed for over 3,600 yards and scored a jaw-dropping 63 touchdowns. That kind of performance doesn't just win games—it leaves people talking about you long after the final whistle. Fans would pack the stands to watch Saquon play, and he never disappointed. Each game felt like a highlight reel in the making.

But it wasn't just his athletic talent that made people love Saquon. He was humble, hardworking, and always quick to credit his teammates for success. He wasn't the kind of player who boasted about his talent. Instead, he let his performance on the field do the talking. Coaches admired his attitude, and teammates admired him as a leader.

As colleges began to notice, Saquon faced a big decision: where would he play next? At first, he committed to Rutgers University, but then something changed. After visiting Penn State University, Saquon knew it was the place for him. The school had a proud football tradition, and Saquon wanted to be part of something special. He flipped his commitment to Penn State, setting the stage for the next chapter in his incredible journey.

High school was where Saquon Barkley proved he had what it took to be a star. He didn't just break records; he inspired everyone around him with his grit, determination, and love for the game. By the time he graduated, it was clear that Saquon wasn't just a high school hero—he was destined for greatness.

College Stardom: Lighting Up the Big Ten

When Saquon Barkley arrived at Penn State University, he didn't just step onto the football field—he exploded onto it like a firework. From the moment he put on his blue and white Nittany

Lions uniform, it was clear that Saquon was something special. He wasn't just a good player; he was a *game-changer*. Fans couldn't take their eyes off him, and defenders couldn't figure out how to stop him.

As a freshman in 2015, Saquon didn't waste any time making an impact. In his second college game, he rushed for 195 yards against Buffalo. Imagine running nearly two football fields in a single game—that's what Saquon did, and he was just getting started. By the end of his first season, he had set Penn State's freshman rushing record with over 1,000 yards. For most players, that would be a career highlight, but for Saquon, it was just the beginning.

Saquon turned it up in his sophomore year—or maybe ten notches. He became the heartbeat of Penn State's offence, electrifying the crowd every time he touched the ball. Whether he was leaping over defenders (yes, *leaping*), breaking tackles, or outrunning everyone on the field, Saquon made the impossible look easy. In 2016, he rushed for 1,496 yards and scored 18 touchdowns, helping Penn State win the Big Ten Championship for the first time in years. His jaw-dropping performance earned him national attention, and people across the country started calling him one of the best players in college football.

But Saquon wasn't just about raw talent—he was also a leader. His teammates looked up to him because he could do amazing things on the field and worked harder than anyone. Whether it was practice, workouts, or film study, Saquon gave it everything. And his dedication inspired the entire team to be better.

Then came his junior season in 2017, and it was nothing short of legendary. Saquon didn't just play football—he put on a show. He opened the season by returning the opening kickoff for a 98-yard touchdown, setting the tone for a year of jaw-dropping highlights. He ran, caught passes, returned kicks, and even threw a touchdown pass! By the end of the season, he had racked up over 2,300 all-purpose yards and 23 touchdowns.

Saquon's performances weren't just about the stats but the moments that made fans leap out of their seats. Like when he hurdled over a Michigan defender as if it were the easiest thing in the world. Or when he broke free for a

92-yard touchdown run that had commentators struggling to find the right words to describe him.

Awards and honours piled up. He won the Paul Hornung Award as the most versatile player in college football, was a two-time Big Ten Offensive Player of the Year, and finished fourth in the Heisman Trophy voting. But through it all, Saquon stayed humble. He never let the spotlight change who he was. He remained the same hardworking, team-first player he'd always been.

By the time Saquon declared for the NFL Draft in 2018, he had left a legacy at Penn State that few could match. He wasn't just one of the best players in school history—he was one of the best players in college football history. Fans knew they had witnessed something special, and Saquon's name would forever be etched in Penn State lore.

College wasn't just a stepping stone for Saquon Barkley—it was where he proved to the world that he was destined for greatness. And as the NFL would soon find out, he was only getting started.

Chapter 3:Rookie of the Year:

Taking the NFL by Storm

When Saquon Barkley entered the NFL in 2018, the hype was sky-high. The New York Giants drafted him second overall, making it clear they believed he wasn't just good—he was *special*. And Saquon didn't disappoint. From the first snap, he played like a man on a mission, proving he was more than ready to shine on the biggest stage.

In his first NFL game, Saquon showed the world exactly what he could do. Facing the Jacksonville Jaguars, one of the league's most formidable defences, he broke free for a jaw-dropping 68-yard touchdown run. It wasn't just a run—it was a statement: "I'm here, and I'm ready." That moment set the tone for one of the best rookie seasons in NFL history.

Week after week, Saquon dazzled fans and confounded defenders. Whether he was sprinting past defenders, breaking tackles like they were made of paper, or leaping over grown men like hurdles, he made every play look like a highlight reel. And he wasn't just running the ball—Saquon proved he could do it all. He caught passes, blocked for his teammates, and even lined up as a receiver, showing his versatility.

By the end of the season, Saquon had put up jaw-dropping numbers: 1,307 rushing yards, 721 receiving yards, and 15 total touchdowns. That's over 2,000 all-purpose yards—more than any other player in the league that year! He also broke records left and right. He set the Giants' rookie rushing record, became the third rookie in NFL history to surpass 2,000 all-purpose yards, and set an NFL record for the most receptions by a rookie running back with 91 catches.

But Saquon wasn't just breaking records; he was winning hearts. His attitude on and off the field showed why he was a fan favourite. Despite all his success, he remained humble and focused. He never took credit for himself, always praising his teammates, coaches, and the fans who supported him. Giants fans knew they had something special—a player who was as great a person as he was an athlete.

Saquon's incredible season didn't go unnoticed. At the end of the year, he was named the NFL Offensive Rookie of the Year, beating out some of the best young players in the league. It was a well-deserved award, but if you asked Saquon, he'd tell you he was just getting started.

What made Saquon's rookie season so special wasn't just the stats or the awards but how he played the game. Every time he touched the ball, it felt like something magical could happen. He brought excitement back to the New York Giants and gave fans hope for the future. Saquon wasn't just a rookie; he was a game-changer, a leader, and a star in the making.

For most players, a season like that would be a career highlight. For Saquon Barkley, it was just the beginning of a legacy that inspires fans of all ages.

Life Off the Field: Family, Fitness, and Fun

While Saquon Barkley is a superstar on the football field, his life off the field is just as inspiring. He's more than just an athlete—he's a family man, a role model, and someone who works hard to give back to others.

At the heart of Saquon's life is his family. He's incredibly close to them, especially his parents, Alibay and Tonya, who raised him to stay humble and grounded no matter how much success he found. His dad taught him about discipline and perseverance, while his mom was his rock, always encouraging him to chase his dreams. Saquon has often said that his family's support keeps him focused, even during tough times.

And then there's his own little family. 2018, Saquon became a dad when his daughter, Jada Clare, was born. For Saquon, fatherhood changed everything. He's said that becoming a dad gave him a whole new perspective on life. Suddenly, it wasn't just about football or personal success—it was about being a role model for Jada. Whether he's pushing her in a stroller, reading her bedtime stories, or sharing sweet father-daughter moments on social media, it's clear that Jada is the centre of his world.

Off the field, Saquon is also a fitness fanatic. He doesn't just work out to stay in shape—he works out to be one of the best athletes in the world. His legendary workouts often go viral, showing him lifting massive weights, sprinting like a track star, and jumping higher than most people imagine. Those powerful legs of his? They didn't just happen by accident. Saquon puts in countless hours in the gym to ensure he's always at the top of his game.

But Saquon isn't all work and no play. He's got a fun side too! He's a big fan of video games and often streams online with other players. Whether dominating in "Madden" (a football video game where he's probably picked as his character!) or joking around with his friends, Saquon knows how to relax and have fun.

Another essential part of Saquon's life is giving back. He understands how much his community shaped him and is passionate about helping others. He's been involved in numerous charity events, donated to important causes, and used his platform to inspire kids to dream big. He wants to show young people that no matter where you come from, you can achieve greatness if you work hard and stay focused.

Saquon Barkley's life off the field reminds us that even the brightest stars are built on a foundation of love, hard work, and kindness. Whether being a loving dad, crushing it in the gym, or giving back to the community, Saquon proves that success is more than touchdowns—it's about making a positive impact wherever you go.

Fun Facts About Saquon Barkley

Here are some fun facts about Saquon Barkley that make him even more remarkable than you thought:

1. Named After a Legend

Saquon's dad named him after a famous boxer, Saad Muhammad because he admired the boxer's toughness. It seems like that fighting spirit runs in the family!

2. A Childhood Idol

Growing up, Saquon was a massive fan of New York Jets running back Curtis Martin. He used to study Martin's moves, and now kids everywhere study *his*.

3. **Cheetah-Like Speed**

Saquon once ran a 40-yard dash in just 4.41 seconds at the NFL Combine. That's about the same speed as a cheetah sprinting...well, maybe not quite, but close enough!

4. Leg Day Champion

Saquon's legs are so strong that he could squat over 500 pounds *while he was still in college*.

That's like lifting a small polar bear—or four giant refrigerators!

5. First Love Was Basketball

Before football, Saquon's first favourite sport was basketball. As a kid, he dreamed of being an NBA player.

6. Hurdle King

Leaping over defenders isn't just something Saquon learned in the NFL. He was hurdling people as early as high school! It's his signature move now.

7. Video Game Superstar

Saquon is so good in the video game *Madden NFL* that even other NFL players complain about how hard it is to stop him. Imagine trying to stop *real* Saquon on the field *and* video game Saquon!

8. Dog Dad

Saquon has a dog named Saint Barkley. Yes, that's right—his dog has his own Instagram page!

9. Record Breaker

During his rookie season, Saquon broke a franchise record with the New York Giants for the most receptions by a running back in a single season. He caught 91 passes!

10. Big Ten Legend

At Penn State, Saquon scored a touchdown five different ways: rushing, receiving, returning kicks, throwing a pass, and even recovering a fumble for a score. Talk about a jack of all trades!

11. Favorite Food

Saquon has a soft spot for sweet treats, especially cookies and cake. After all, even superstars need a cheat day sometimes.

12. Nickname Alert

Some fans call him "SaQuads" because of his insanely muscular legs. Others stick with the classic "Super Saquon." Either way, the nicknames are as impressive as his moves.

Saquon Barkley isn't just an incredible athlete—he's also full of surprises. Whether he's leaping over defenders, scoring touchdowns, or spoiling his dog, there's always something fun and fascinating about him!

Football Drills Inspired by Saquon

If you want to train like Saquon Barkley (or at least try to), here are some football drills inspired by his explosive speed, powerful legs, and quick feet. These drills won't guarantee you'll leap over defenders or outrun the entire team, but they'll help you build strength, agility, and coordination like a true superstar!

1. Cone Agility Drills

Saquon's ability to change direction in a split second is legendary, and cone drills are perfect for developing that quickness.

- Set up cones in a zigzag or triangle pattern.

- Sprint to the first cone, then quickly cut (change direction) to the next cone.

- Focus on staying low and keeping your steps short and fast.

- Bonus: Time yourself and try to beat your record!

2. Box Jumps for Explosive Power

Those powerful leaps Saquon uses to hurdle defenders? They come from explosive leg strength, and box jumps are the way to build it.

- Find a sturdy box or platform (start with something low and work your way up).
- Stand before the box, squat slightly, and explode upward, landing softly on top.
- Step down and repeat for 10–12 reps.
- Tip: Focus on jumping straight up and using your arms to help lift you.

3. Ladder Drills for Quick Feet

Saquon's feet move so fast it's like they're dancing! Ladder drills are great for improving footwork and coordination.

- Lay a speed ladder on the ground or draw one with chalk.

- Practice different foot patterns:

  - High knees through each square.

  - Two feet in each square.

  - Side shuffles down the ladder.

- The goal is to move quickly while staying in control.

4. Resistance Sprints for Speed

Try adding resistance to your sprints to develop the breakaway speed Saquon is famous for.

- Use a resistance band or a sledge, or even have a partner lightly hold you back with a towel.

- Sprint forward as hard as possible for 10–20 yards, focusing on driving your knees high and pumping your arms.

- Repeat for 5–6 sets with rest in between.

5. One-Legged Squats for Balance and Strength

Saquon's insane balance and leg strength let him power through tackles and stay on his feet. One-legged squats (or pistol squats) are great for building the same kind of stability.

- Stand on one leg and extend the other leg straight out in front of you.

- Slowly lower your body as far as possible, then push back up.

- Hold onto a chair or wall for support if it's too harsh.

6. Medicine Ball Throws for Core Power

Saquon's strong core helps him absorb hits and stay explosive. Medicine ball drills are perfect for developing that same power.

- Grab a medicine ball and stand a few feet from a wall or partner.

- Twist your torso and throw the ball as hard as possible to one side, then catch it and repeat on the other.

- Do 8–10 throws on each side.

7. Hurdle Drills for Jumping Ability

Want to leap over defenders like Saquon? Practice your vertical and horizontal jumping skills with hurdles.

- Set up a row of low hurdles or cones.

- Jump over each one, focusing on tucking your knees to your chest.

- Land softly and immediately jump to the next one.

- Repeat for 3–4 sets of 10 jumps.

8. Catch-and-Run Drills

Saquon isn't just a runner—he's also a fantastic receiver. Work on your ability to catch and accelerate.

- Have a partner toss you the ball while you move.
- Focus on catching it cleanly and bursting into a sprint as soon as it's in your hands.
- Practice cutting around cones or defenders after the catch to simulate game situations.

9. Tire Pulls for Raw Power

For a workout that screams Saquon's strength, try pulling tyres.

- Attach a rope or harness to a heavy tyre.

- Drag the tyre forward for 20–30 yards as fast as possible.

- This builds serious lower-body strength and explosive power.

10. Shadow Running for Vision and Decision-Making

Saquon's ability to "see" the field and make split-second decisions is a key part of his game. Shadow running helps improve those instincts.

- Have a coach or friend hold a football and stand a few yards before you.

- They'll point in different directions, and your job is to react instantly and run that way.

- Add cones or "defenders" to simulate dodging obstacles.

Saquon's Training Mindset

Saquon doesn't just train hard—he trains smart. Remember to focus on proper technique, stay consistent, and push yourself without overdoing it. Most importantly, always keep that Saquon-like mindset: believe in yourself, stay humble, and have fun while you work toward greatness!

Conclusion: Run Hard, Dream Big Like Saquon Barkley!

Saquon Barkley's story is one of perseverance, passion, and purpose. From his early days in The Bronx, where big dreams were born, to his rise as one of the most electrifying players in the NFL, Saquon has shown that greatness isn't just about talent—it's about hard work, heart, and a determination never to give up. His journey proves that challenges are just stepping stones to success.

In Pennsylvania, Saquon learned the value of pushing through adversity. He wasn't always the strongest or the fastest, but he trained relentlessly to turn his weaknesses into strengths. By the time he reached high school, he wasn't just playing football—he was redefining it. At Penn State, he didn't just shine; he became a beacon of hope and excitement for fans everywhere, dazzling with his ability to turn ordinary plays into unforgettable moments. And when he entered the NFL, Saquon didn't just meet expectations—he exceeded them, breaking records, winning awards, and becoming a role model for kids dreaming of their big break.

But what makes Saquon truly special isn't just what he does on the field—it's who he is off the field. He's a family man, a teammate, and a leader. He humbly carries himself, always remembering where he came from and the people who helped him. His love for his daughter, Jada, shines brightly, reminding us that even the biggest stars are grounded by what truly matters: love, family, and giving back. Saquon's dedication to his community, his kindness to fans, and his commitment to inspiring others prove that being great isn't just about winning games but improving the world around you.

Saquon's career is far from over; the best may still come. But no matter what the future holds, his legacy is already cemented. He's not just a football player—he's a symbol of what's possible when you combine talent with effort, determination with discipline, and heart with hope. Saquon Barkley has inspired millions with his incredible journey, and his story reminds us all that dreams can come true if you work for them, believe in yourself, and never quit.

So whether you're a young athlete chasing your dreams, a fan who loves the game, or someone looking for a reason to believe in the power of hard work, Saquon's story proves that greatness is within reach. All it takes is a little courage, effort, and the willingness to accept every challenge in stride—just like Saquon Barkley.

www.ingramcontent.com/pod-product-compliance
Lightning Source LLC
Chambersburg PA
CBHW071245180325
23673CB00036B/509